The Book of Answers: The Expert's Guide To Navigating College Admissions

The Book of Answers: The Expert's Guide To Navigating College Admissions

REVISED EDITION

**Wesley Berkowitz, Ph.D. and
Jamie L. Reich, M.S., P.D.**

ISBN: 1548307564
ISBN 13: 9781548307561
Library of Congress Control Number: 2017912366
CreateSpace Independent Publishing Platform
North Charleston, South Carolina

This book has been a labor of love, and we dedicate it to the many students and families who have placed their trust in us over the years. We feel truly blessed to have had the opportunity to be invited into their lives at this exciting/daunting time of the college planning and application process. We hope that through this book, we will continue to guide students and their families, past, present, and future.

Heartfelt thanks to Karen Bartscherer, Jackie Nealon, Susan Miller, and A-List Education contributors Scott Farber, Michelle Richards, Anna Marie Smith and Edward Smallwood for their indelible contributions, and to Scott Reich for his commitment to this project, steadfast support, and tireless efforts.

And, most of all, for the source of our inspiration and love, our families: Adam, Amanda, Andrew, Beverly, Brittany, Carole, Eddie, Edward, Emelia Morgan, Ethan, Evelyn, Howie, Ilissa, Jesse, Leslie, Michael, Randi, and Scott.

About the Authors

Jamie L. Reich

Jamie L. Reich, a native of Long Island, holds a bachelor of arts in psychology, sociology, and education, cum laude, from Washington University in St. Louis, Missouri; a master of science in education with distinction with a specialization in counselor education from Hofstra University in Uniondale, New York; and a New York State public school teacher permanent certification in school counseling. In addition, she holds a professional diploma with high honors in marriage and family therapy from Hofstra University.

Jamie is a professional member of the Independent Educational Consultants Association and is a member of the National Association for College Admission

Counseling, Nassau Counselors' Association, and the New York State Association for College Admission Counseling. Additionally, she has served as director of college advising services for a prestigious New York–based education company. In an effort to remain current, she visits college campuses and meets with admissions officers and academic deans on a regular basis. Jamie has successfully guided hundreds of students and their parents through the exciting yet stressful college application process. She works closely with students on college selection, creating a stellar résumé, brainstorming essays, building interview skills, and assisting with deferral/waitlist strategies as well as transfer applications. She provides early guidance for ninth, tenth, and eleventh graders in academic planning, extracurricular activities including community-service efforts, and summer planning. She also provides assistance with graduate school applications and essay brainstorming. Jamie prides herself on the trust that clients have placed in her, as she becomes the go-to person for siblings and friends. The lasting relationships she builds with clients endure well beyond the college-application process.

Spending time with family and friends brings Jamie her greatest joy.

Wesley Berkowitz

Born and raised in New York City, Wesley has a bachelor's degree in elementary education / social science, a master's degree with distinction in counselor education, a professional diploma in counseling, and a family therapy certificate, all earned at Hofstra University in Uniondale, New York. He also has a professional diploma in educational administration from Long Island University / C. W. Post in Brookville, New York; a bachelor's in counseling and guidance at Duke University in Durham, North Carolina; and a PhD in counseling psychology from the Union Institute & University in Cincinnati, Ohio.

He was a school counselor at the Wheatley School (grades eight–twelve) in Old Westbury, New York, for thirty-three years, where his primary responsibilities involved personal, academic, career, and college counseling. Over the course of his career, he has helped thousands of students and parents navigate the college admissions process from start to finish. His relationships with students and parents have been so positive that he is often sought out by his now-adult former students to assist their children with college admission.

Currently, he lives on the North Shore of Long Island. He is happily married and the very proud father of two wonderful sons.

Additional Contributors

K̲aren Bartscherer, freelance writer and editor, has taught English at the Wheatley School in Old Westbury, New York, and at Adelphi University in Garden City, New York.

Susan Miller worked for thirty-three years in the East Williston School District in Old Westbury, New York, and is currently a special-education administrator in the Locust Valley School District, Locust Valley, New York.

Dr. Jacquelyn Nealon serves as chief of staff and vice president of enrollment, campus life, and communications for Long Island University, Greenvale, New York.

Jacquelyn is an expert in expanding college affordability, financial aid, admissions, and enrollment management.

Mark Kowalsky is a college counselor at the Schechter School of Long Island, having educated teenagers and their families for almost forty-one years. A former English teacher at Forest Hills High School, guidance counselor at the Wheatley School in Long Island's East Williston School District, from which he retired after fourteen years, and college admissions counselor for New York Institute of Technology, Mark brings a wealth of experience and expertise to the college admissions process. He holds a BA in English from CUNY Brooklyn College, an MA in English education from New York University, and an MS in school counseling from St. John's University. He has a certification in administration from New York University and has extensive coursework and experience in art history, a field that inspires him as his students continue to enrich his life. He is actively involved in many professional organizations and college admissions conferences. Mark has visited hundreds of colleges throughout his long career and built a network of colleagues and college admissions counselors, and as a result has kept abreast of all components of the college process.

Jason Stadler graduated from Queens College with a degree in sociology and earned an MBA at Washington University's Olin School of Business, distinguishing himself as a Beta Gamma Sigma Honor Society inductee. During his graduate studies, Jason served as a teaching assistant in various entrepreneurial, leadership, and management courses and started two acclaimed education companies, Future U and Test Experience. He also served as a mentor to the Next Step, a start-up providing unique interview preparatory services to potential medical school applicants. Prior to starting his companies, Jason was a summer associate in the investment management division of Goldman Sachs. He also worked at Advantage Testing for six years, where he tutored hundreds of students and developed a strong teaching reputation in the New York community. Jason prepared students for the MCAT, PSAT, SAT I, SAT II (bio, Math 1C, chemistry, physics, and writing), ACT, SSAT, and GRE. Prior to his time at Advantage Testing, Jason served as a director of an educational program at the Hispanic Counseling Center that taught science, mathematics, and English to economically disadvantaged children. Jason is an avid athlete who played professional basketball both internationally and in the United States. He has also quarterbacked a team to the national flag football championship.

Introduction

There are many college books on the market today, but unfortunately, most tend to be bulky and not user friendly when it comes to answering questions about applying to college. We decided to write a book that speaks directly to you, the parent, about the nuts and bolts of what to expect, and to help navigate the many facets of the college admission process.

Over the years, parents and students have consistently asked us the kinds of questions that are neither typically nor readily found in most college books. Our handbook is a compilation of answers to the most-often-asked questions as each step of applying to college unfolds. Each chapter covers an important component of the process and provides answers in an easy-to-understand format. It is a single all-in-one resource that offers a compendium of information that catalogs the subject matter, enabling readily accessible answers.

Contents

Standardized Tests (PSAT/SAT and ACT)

Standardized Testing Overview

I n March 2016, the substance and format of the SAT exam changed—and with that, so did the world of test prep! While change typically heightens a student's levels of stress and anxiety, the changes that were made should in fact be welcome news to all test takers (and the parents of all test takers!).

In the past, the SAT and ACT exams were so different from one another that it was incredibly challenging for students to prepare for both—especially during an already difficult junior year. The major stumbling block for most students was the SAT's focus on difficult and obscure vocabulary words, which they were forced to memorize and later understand on the exam in the context of reading passages and sentence-completion questions. This required countless hours of memorization exercises, but none of this work was helpful in test prep for the ACT exam, which did not have the same focus on vocabulary.

Fortunately, the new SAT exam does not emphasize vocabulary as much as the old exam did, and the content is similar to that of the ACT exam. As a result, a student's studies can apply to both exams, which minimizes wasted effort and expands the student's ability to prepare for both exams at the same time.

How else has the SAT changed?

The College Board is the body responsible for the SAT exam, and the new SAT exam is basically the College Board's version of the ACT. In addition to eliminating some of the obscure vocabulary words, the SAT no longer contains sentence-completion questions or point deductions for incorrect answers, and the maximum score amount is no longer 2400.

The new SAT contains four sections: evidence-based reading, writing and language (with an optional essay), math with no calculator, and math with a calculator permitted. The reading and writing and language sections are worth a combined 800, and the two math sections are also worth a combined 800, for a maximum score of 1600—like the "old days." The College Board has also incorporated charts and graphs into each of the sections on occasion to mimic the science section of the ACT.

Should my child consider the SAT or ACT?

Since colleges not only accept both exams but assign them equal weight in their application processes, and since the exams test similar concepts, we believe that students should consider taking both exams. Absent a compelling reason to the contrary, however, we believe most students should focus their early preparation on the ACT.

There are two major reasons for doing so:

- We believe that the best way to prepare for an exam is to work with official preparatory materials. Since the substance and format of the SAT is so new, there are only seven official SAT exams that students can use as practice tests.

This pales in comparison to the more than fifty official exams that students can use to prepare for the ACT. Even if your child is a stronger SAT test taker, the dearth of such practice materials makes it difficult to fully prepare for the exam the way students can for the ACT.

- The ACT contains sections that require students to complete questions in less time than that provided on the SAT. Take the reading section, for example, which both exams offer. The ACT offers students eight minutes and forty-five seconds to both read the passage and answer the related questions; the SAT, which contains a passage of similar length, gives students thirteen minutes to complete a similar task. As a result, preparing for the ACT forces students to practice reading and answering questions at a faster pace, meaning that it would be easier for them to transition from studying for the ACT to the SAT than vice versa. It's always easier to be given more time than to grow accustomed to a particular exam pace and then be forced to work more quickly.

Having said the above, we must remember that the test-prep process is different for each student. What works for one student may not work for another. The takeaway here is that we should encourage students to embrace the similarities of these exams and not immediately dismiss an exam because of a preconceived notion. More options are better than fewer options!

What type of student may do better on the SAT?

It is difficult to determine what type of student will do better on the SAT. Every student has different strengths and weaknesses. Because the timing on the SAT is a little less challenging than the timing on the ACT, it is logical to think that a slower test taker or a slower reader will do better on the SAT. We have found that indeed sometimes this is the case, but other times it is not. When you compare both exams closely, the differences become more pronounced.

Let's take a look at the different parts of the test. First, let's analyze reading. The major challenge of the ACT is the timing. As we mentioned earlier, students have to read lengthy passages (seventy-five to one hundred lines) and answer ten questions in eight minutes and forty-five seconds. This isn't easy. The more comforting part is that the questions are fairly straightforward and do not require deep critical thinking about the subtleties of the passages. The answer choices, for the most part, are obviously right or wrong. Students can do well if they are able to remember the content of the passage or are able to go back and find the information directly in the passage.

The SAT, on the other hand, is more forgiving with the timing. Students have to read seventy-five to one hundred lines per passage and answer ten or eleven questions in thirteen minutes. That's an extra four minutes and fifteen seconds as compared to the timing on the ACT.

The questions on the SAT, however, require deeper critical thinking and inferencing skills. Correct answers are less clear. The SAT reading section emphasizes more critical reading rather than reading comprehension. A student who struggles in this area will have difficulty in this section. In addition, the level of vocabulary used in the passages and in the questions and answers is more sophisticated than that of the ACT. So if your child is a strong, fast reader, your child should be able to do well on either reading section. If your child is a weaker or slower reader, your child will probably find the ACT easier than the SAT, but the timing on the ACT might be too much of an obstacle to overcome. If your child is a strong but slow reader, the SAT might be a better test. In all cases, proper training and constant practice can improve timing and performance.

Should my child take the writing section?

The writing section for both the SAT and ACT is optional, meaning that a student can sign up for the exam with or without taking the writing section. There is an additional fee to take the writing section, so many students opt to take the test without it for financial reasons. Many schools do require the writing section, though. So unless your child is 100 percent sure that the schools to which your child is applying do not require writing, we recommend all students take the exam with writing. But don't worry too much about the writing score. It is a separate score from the overall score (graded on a scale from one to twelve), and most colleges that require the writing section don't use it to make academic judgments.

Is there still an "experimental" section on the SAT?

The College Board website states, "To allow for pretesting, some students taking the SAT with no essay will take a fifth, twenty-minute section. Any section of the SAT may contain both optional and pretest items." Pretest items are so-called experimental questions that do not count toward your child's score and are used so that the College Board can test questions before using them on an actual exam. From the wording on the College Board website, it seems as if any section could have these experimental questions. It is our belief, however, that they are only in the fifth section and that the College Board uses that specific wording with the hope that students will take that section seriously. If not, statistically analyzing that section would be futile.

What is the PSAT, and should my child take it?

The PSAT is basically a shorter version of the SAT and is a practice exam: colleges never see the scores, and the exam does not "count" in the college application process. The PSAT is given in October of your child's junior year and is entirely optional. For students who perform at the highest levels, there are national merit scholarships available, but these are only for students who score in the top percentiles. For everyone else, the PSAT is simply an opportunity to get some practice for the SAT—not only the form and substance of the exam but also the real-life test conditions. If your child takes the PSAT in tenth grade, it will not count toward scholarship competitions.

Your child will subsequently get a copy of the exam with an answer key, which will clearly show your child's strengths and weaknesses. We recommend your child take the exam, as it provides a good learning opportunity with no downside. No matter what your child's PSAT score is, there is always room to improve!

Should my child take the PSAT in tenth grade or wait until eleventh grade?

Taking the test just two months into the sophomore year means your child will not have the benefit of the natural learning curve that typically occurs between tenth and eleventh grades. Many tenth-graders have not sufficiently covered important mathematics topics so early in the school year to be able to do their best on the test. Also, even though it's a practice test, if your child scores poorly on it, will that cause stress, impact self-confidence, or create undue anxiety? Keep in mind that only the test scores from eleventh grade are used for scholarship-program competitions. The decision of whether to take the PSAT in tenth grade should be considered carefully.

Do colleges consider the ACT to be inferior, equal, or superior to the SAT?

The SAT and ACT are regarded equally by colleges and universities and are virtually interchangeable. Some colleges will use the ACT plus writing in lieu of both the SAT and the SAT subject tests. If your child scores better on one of the tests, then there's no need to submit the scores on the other test. If your child scores equally well on both the SAT and ACT, then consider submitting both the scores to demonstrate consistency.

Is it a good idea to take both the SAT and the ACT?

We recommend taking a diagnostic test for both the SAT and ACT to determine which test is a better fit for your child's learning style.

What's the latest my child should take the SAT? ACT? SAT subject tests?

Your child should take the SAT and/or ACT in the spring of junior year, and, unless the score was exceptionally high, retake whichever test had the higher score in the fall of senior year. Generally, students take the SAT in March or May of their junior year and a second time in October or November of senior year. The SAT can additionally be taken in August. The ACT should also be taken in the spring, and if a student wishes to take it a second time, it's available in July and again in September. As for SAT subject tests, they should be taken in May or June, depending on when the high-school or college-level course is over. Juniors in high school who are enrolled in Advanced Placement courses should consider taking the subject tests in May.

How many times should my child take the SAT or ACT?

Unless your child achieves exceptional scores on the first try, it makes sense to take the SAT or ACT a second time. Research indicates that taking the test more than twice does not significantly increase the overall score.

Nevertheless, if there is one particular component that is a consistent Achilles' heel, then your child should take it one last time to see if the desired score can be achieved.

How does superscoring work?

Superscoring takes into account the highest score of each of your child's sections, regardless of test date. It is the policy of many colleges to use the students' best scores on each section of the SAT and ACT (whichever your child opts to submit to colleges) from multiple test administrations, rather than scores from one test. Many colleges require students to submit all of their scores, but they typically consider your child's highest scores as representative of your child's true capability. We recommend that your child check each college's official website to determine whether they superscore one or both standardized tests.

What is Score Choice?

Score Choice is an option offered by the College Board to help alleviate stress by allowing students to submit to colleges only the scores they choose to send. Score

Choice is by test date for the SAT, and by individual test for SAT subject tests.

Are there colleges that don't require the ACT or SAT?

Yes, there are some colleges that are Test Optional, meaning that students do not have to submit either standardized test. Colleges may require some alternative in lieu of the exams such as an interview, an extra essay, or a graded paper from school. The website www.fairtest.org gives more information about colleges that forgo standardized tests.

Are the SAT and ACT easier on some test dates than others?

Although many people believe this is true, there is no evidence to support it. The College Board and ACT do all that they can to ensure that the level of difficulty is standardized among all tests that are administered throughout the year.

Applications

What are the most important criteria in college admissions?

The college admissions process is an art, not a science. Admissions officers weigh many criteria: test scores, GPA, letters of recommendation, extracurricular activities, the required and supplemental college essays and interviews (when recommended). Additionally, a number of colleges take geographic location into account. Depending on the school, GPA and test scores have a significant impact. They offer an indication of how ready a student is for college and how well the student will be able to handle the academic rigor of college classes. Even so, leadership and community involvement can play a major role. Admissions officers want to see how a student is involved in the community in high school and what that student will bring to the college campus. This is a great question to ask during campus tours and information sessions.

What are the components of my child's college application file?

Your child's guidance counselor will submit a high-school transcript, a school profile, and a letter of recommendation. In addition, many schools will require recommendations from teachers (usually two). Increasingly, colleges require that teacher and guidance counselor recommendations be submitted through Naviance, if the school uses this software. Your child is responsible for submitting the completed application with all required essays, application fees, and résumé (if required). Your child must report standardized test scores directly from www.act.org or www.collegeboard.com.

What is the difference between the Common Application and the Universal College Application?

The nonprofit organization behind the Common Application offers a standard application form that is accepted by more than 550 colleges and universities. This application enables students to complete personal data and upload a personal statement essay, then submit this information to multiple colleges simultaneously.

Your child should go to www.commonapp.org and follow the prompts to create an account using your child's e-mail and password.

The for-profit Universal College Application is accepted by more than forty colleges and universities and was also created to save time for students by enabling them to submit the same application to any of the participating colleges. Most of the schools participating in the Universal College Application also accept the Common Application.

My child is having a problem with the Common Application. Is there someone to contact for help?

There is no phone support available. All technical support is done by e-mail through the Help Center, which is located on the Common Application. (Note: Add this address to your child's address book so tech support responses will not go to the spam folder: appsupport@ commonapp.org.) Many questions can be answered directly through links at the Applicant Help Center and related searches on the Knowledgebase tab. These can be reached from a button on the commonapp.org homepage.

Writing a Résumé

Does my child really need to have a résumé?

While many colleges do not require students to submit résumés, it can be helpful, especially if your child is applying to the more competitive colleges. In one organized, succinct document, your child can share detailed information about academic honors, awards, extracurricular activities, private lessons, work experience, travel, community service, and other appropriate events. Some interviewers will use information from the résumé as an icebreaker during an alumni or on-campus interview.

Please note that a résumé will only supplement, not replace, the activities section of the Common Application. Students can use the additional information section of the Common Application (underneath writing) to elaborate on activities of importance or to cut and paste a résumé. Some colleges may allow for an upload of a résumé in their individual questions sections.

What's the best format to use for the résumé?

A résumé should be no longer than two pages. Topics should be in bold type, and items within each category should be listed in chronological order. Admissions officers want to see the hours per week and weeks per year that your child was involved, so include those as well.

What makes a résumé stand out?

An especially strong GPA or standardized test score, although noted on other documents, is worth repeating on a résumé. Also, any title in a school or community organization (e.g., president, captain, treasurer) that has been earned should be listed in bold font. Any special talents recognized in or out of school are important to highlight as well. Finally, any summer activities of substance (e.g., college courses and community service) should be included. As with every other document sent to a prospective college, make sure spelling and grammar are perfect!

Is there anything not to list on a résumé?

Any brief or superficial activities should not be listed. For example, colleges are not interested in knowing that your child likes playing handball, watching action movies, or playing video games. Colleges are interested in substance, not fluff.

Are Social Security numbers required on the résumés?

A Social Security number is not necessary, and listing it could make your child vulnerable to identity theft. With date of birth, e-mail address, home address, and phone number listed on the résumé, there's more than enough identifying information should the document inadvertently become separated from the rest of the application.

Decision Plans

What is the difference between Early Decision, Early Action, and Single-Choice or Restrictive Early Action?

Early Decision: ED is an optional plan offered by many colleges in which students make a commitment to a first-choice institution where, if admitted, they definitely will enroll. While pursuing admission under an Early Decision plan, students may apply to other institutions, but may have only one Early Decision application pending at any time. Early Decision deadlines are usually November 1 (some schools are October 15 or November 15), and decisions are released in mid-December. This is a binding decision/contract that is signed by the student (and parent) at the time of the application. If admitted, all other applications that have been submitted must be withdrawn. Obviously, careful research, campus visits, interviews, financial factors, and satisfactory completion of standardized tests prior to application are critical.

Early Action: For colleges offering this option, students apply by November 1 (some schools are November 15) and receive decision notification between mid-December and mid-January. Early Action is not a binding contract; however, students should thoroughly research all of the educational opportunities offered, visit campuses, take alumni or on-campus interviews, complete SAT and/or ACT with writing tests, and consider financial factors prior to applying Early Action.

Single-Choice or Restrictive Early Action: Applications must be submitted prior to November 1 and decisions are rendered in mid-December. This is a nonbinding decision plan; however, students should thoroughly research all of their educational options, visit campuses, take interviews, complete all standardized testing, and consider financial factors prior to applying.

The student cannot apply Early Action or Early Decision to any other private institutions; however, application to public institutions or colleges outside the United States, provided that admission is not binding, is acceptable. Certain schools that utilize this decision plan have additional requirements on applications, and it is your child's obligation to understand the specifics pertaining to each college.

The student may apply to an Early Decision II program after receiving a decision from the Single-Choice Early Action program. If admitted through another college's Early Decision II binding program, your child must withdraw the application from the Single-Choice Early Action school.

Early Decision II: This option refers to those colleges that offer two Early Decision opportunities. While the deadline for ED I is typically November 1 or 15, the deadline for ED II is usually in early to mid-January. ED II is for students who either fall in love with a school past the ED I deadline or were deferred or denied from their first-choice college, and the ED II college is now their new first choice. ED II also benefits students who are late bloomers by allowing the college to view their midyear grades before making a decision.

If my child applies Early Decision (ED) or Early Action (EA) to a college, should my child send them first-quarter grades?

Yes, if one of these three conditions apply:

- The college requires them.
- The student maintains a strong academic profile.
- The student has improved upon past performance.

Is there a benefit to applying EA or ED?

Statistics demonstrate that a higher percentage of students who apply ED or EA are accepted to the incoming freshman class. That being said, the applicant pool is different, since these students are committing to attend, if they are admitted. Acceptance rates vary year to year depending on the number of applicants and the strength of the pool. Most schools do not have a quota for any of their decision plans, so the applicant's strengths and quality of application are more important than the choice of decision plan. One reason schools admit more students in ED or EA is that it will increase their matriculation rate, which reflects well on their admission statistics. The most important consideration must always be whether the university is your child's absolute top choice, and whether your child will make a commitment to enroll if accepted.

What does it mean to be "deferred"?

An applicant can only be deferred in Early Action and Early Decision. This means that the admissions committee has not made a decision about acceptance yet; your child remains in the applicant pool for reconsideration during the review of applications for regular admissions. If your child is deferred, any significant new information should be reported to the Undergraduate Admissions office in an effort to enhance your child's chances of ultimately being accepted, including awards received, new employment or community-service endeavors, and new positions/titles held in activities in or out of school. Many schools will request midyear grades before making an admissions decision and even after an offer of admission has been made. These grades can make or break an admissions decision. Students must inform their school counselor when these documents are requested. In addition, keeping in touch with an admissions officer and confirming that the school is still the top choice will only benefit the student's application.

What is Rolling Admission?

Rolling Admission enables the student to submit an admissions application at any time. The institutions will process all credentials at the time they are received, without regard to a specific application due date. An admissions decision is then typically rendered within a four- to ten-week period.

What is Regular Decision?

Regular Decision generally refers to the traditional admissions timetable. Typically, students submit their applications and supporting documents by January 1 or 15 and will receive an admissions decision in early to mid-April.

Some schools have Priority Admission Deadlines. What are these?

Some schools indicate that, in order to be considered for scholarships and honors programs, students must submit applications by a deadline that is earlier than their traditional deadlines. For example, if you apply by November 1 to the University of Maryland, you will automatically be considered for their Honors Programs. Check admissions deadline timetables on the school's website.

What does it mean to be "waitlisted"?

Waitlists refer specifically to regular and rolling decision plans. Colleges and universities will postpone making a final decision about some potentially admissible candidates. Once the school has received notifications from admitted students who, by accepting offers at other colleges, have created openings for students on their waitlists, the colleges and universities revisit their waitlisted students and make their final decisions about these candidates. While some waitlists are ranked, others are not. If a school overenrolled one year, they may waitlist and later admit those students the following year in order to keep their matriculation numbers on target. There is no definite way to know if a school will take students off a waitlist each year. Some schools, especially the most selective, may not even go to their waitlist.

If my child is waitlisted, what can be done to strengthen the application?

If the desire to attend the school is serious and strong, keep the admissions officer well informed and confirm that your child will attend if admitted. Additionally, your child must maintain strong grades and report any and all positive tidbits of information that have occurred since the application was filed. It won't hurt to arrange another campus visit, perhaps even interview with an on-campus admissions officer and sit in on classes. All of these extras demonstrate to the college a clear commitment and interest.

Can my child appeal a denial decision?

Only some schools allow you to appeal a denial. Your child can appeal a denial by substantiating any new information that has occurred since the application was submitted. It is a difficult process to win, but if being admitted to a particular college is important, this might be worth a shot. Realistically, however, students should consider looking more carefully at the colleges to which they have already been offered acceptances because they may find alternatives to their "dream" school.

What happens if my child gets accepted Early Decision and decides later to attend another college? Is there any penalty?

When an ED application is filed, a binding contract is entered into with the school, stating that if admission is granted, your child will attend. Your child cannot back out of this contract after applying to a school Early Decision. This is precisely why your child needs to think long and hard BEFORE filing an ED application.

My child's favorite college doesn't offer Early Decision. How does my child let them know they're the number-one choice and my child will attend if admitted?

Your child should let them know on the application supplement. Your child may also e-mail the admissions office informing them of those intentions. It would be more personal if your child sent an e-mail to the regional admissions officer. If your child cannot find out who the regional admissions officer is, e-mail the school and ask to have the letter added to the application file.

The Application Process

How many colleges should my child apply to?

In most cases, about eight colleges is a good number, including safety, target, and reach schools. A safety school is one in which your child's GPA and standardized test scores are well above the publicized admission criteria. A target school is one to which your child has a fifty-fifty shot of acceptance, and where your child's GPA and standardized test scores are within the requirements of the school for acceptance. A reach school is exactly that—a reach. Taking a realistic reach is a good move. There are certainly other factors that come into play for admission, especially if your child is on the cusp for admission. They include high-school activities, leadership roles, teacher recommendations, and of course essays. If there is a wide discrepancy between the math and reading sections of your child's standardized tests, your child should probably apply to more than ten schools to present the broadest range of possibilities for acceptance.

Is the deadline for applying the postmark date or the actual date?

Since colleges now expect applications to be submitted online (unless otherwise indicated on the application), the deadline is obviously the actual date, at 11:59 p.m. YOUR local time. For applications that must be sent through the mail, play it safe and assume that the application must be received by the stated due date.

Should my child work with a private counselor, or is a school counselor a good option?

It all depends. Is your child a motivated self-starter who will utilize the services offered by the high school? For instance, does your child plan to ask an English teacher to proofread and critique the college essays? If that's going to be the strategy, then it's unlikely that a private counselor will be needed. If your child feels either insecure or overwhelmed or both, though, the extra support provided by a private college counselor in navigating the college admissions process may well be worth the investment.

An independent educational consultant or college adviser is a valued resource for applicants and parents who want a more individualized, personal, and caring approach to the highly stressful college planning and application process. So much of finding the right "fit" for the applicant involves spending the time to really get to know a student and determine what might be the right college setting. Independent educational consultants have insight into the colleges because they spend a considerable amount of time touring campuses and their surrounding area and meeting with admissions officers. Additionally, they regularly attend conferences and workshops to keep up with trends. As a result, private college advisers provide assistance with clients by providing objective advice throughout the entire college application process.

Should my child fill out the Common Application ("Common App") or use the school's individual application?

If applying to a Common Application member school, your child should use the Common App. If a school offers both the Common App and its own application, it will not have a preference for either application type, but choosing to use the Common App for as many schools as possible will keep students from duplicating efforts.

Should my child send in any supplemental information?

If a college or university wants other writing samples, résumés, or graded papers, they will request those as uploaded documents in the writing supplement of the Common Application. Additionally, if new information about your child becomes available at any time (e.g., awards and position of leadership), be sure to inform the colleges about it. Keeping in touch demonstrates continued interest in attending that school.

My child has submitted the Common Application and wants to make a change. Is it possible?

On the Common Application, you can make unlimited edits to an already submitted application before the second is submitted, with the exception of the 650-word-maximum essay. This essay should not be tailored to one specific school, as those supplemental essays will be found on the writing supplement of the Common Application. If your child needs to make major changes to an application, it is possible to e-mail the new document to the school and ask to have it uploaded to the application.

How does a school's weighting of grades factor into the GPA?

Many high schools have different weighting systems, and others do not weight at all. Along with the transcript, the guidance counselor will send a high-school profile describing the courses that your child took and the weighting system. Colleges have a method by which they determine how to equalize grading systems to accommodate the differences. Since some schools do not recalculate GPAs, they will look to see if your child has taken the most difficult classes offered.

Will homeschooling help or hurt my child's chances for being accepted to colleges?

Nearly 1 percent of students living in the United States are homeschooled. Because admissions policies vary from school to school, college-bound students must understand the individual requirements of each school to which they intend to apply. Deadlines must be adhered to and a detailed account of your child's academic coursework must be prepared for submission. As a home-schooled student, your child is required to verify academic expertise through standardized tests: the SAT I, ACT, and SAT subject tests. Additionally, your child must submit evaluations from someone other than you, the parent, even if you are the primary instructor. Leadership and community-service efforts are important components of your child's application.

What is a gap year?

A gap year is an intermission from traditional education. It usually refers to a student taking time off between graduating from high school and entering college. It is a time to gain life experience and maturity in a setting other than the academic environment. This may be done in a structured environment and can awaken the learning process in a different venue. While this can be a positive experience, the lag in educational continuity can sometimes make it difficult for the student to get back into a frame of mind conducive to an educational setting. Most students taking a gap year after gradua-tion will apply to colleges before graduating, and then defer admission for a year. (Not all schools allow a stu-dent to defer, so check with the colleges to learn about their policies.)

What is the difference between a college and a university?

A college refers to a program that confers a bachelor's degree. All students of a college are undergraduates. Some colleges are part of a larger institution (univer-sity) and others are entities unto themselves, devoted to a particular discipline, including but not limited to engineering, business, and arts and sciences.

A university is an educational institution that com-bines one or more colleges, often conferring graduate degrees, including, but not limited to, MD, DDS, MBA, JD, and PhD. For example, the University of Pennsylvania is the umbrella name of a university that comprises sev-eral colleges including The College (Arts and Sciences), Wharton (the Business School), and the School of Engineering.

What is a community college?

A community college is a two-year school where students receive college credits. Some students attend community college if they do not have the necessary grades or test scores for a four-year college. Other students attend a community college to figure out what they want to do in life before spending a lot of money and later transfer to a four-year college. Additionally, students might opt to attend a community college if they are planning to go to school part time while also working. Community colleges accept students of a wide academic and socioeconomic range. Credits at a community college cost significantly less than they do at a four-year college.

Advanced Placement (AP) Courses/Exams

What is an AP course?

Advanced Placement courses are considered to be college-level courses in terms of scope and content. They are offered through high schools and in conjunction with the College Board and cover a wide range of subjects. AP courses should prepare students for the AP exams administered in May.

Should an AP score of 3 be sent to colleges during the application process?

Yes. Although colleges typically offer advanced placement or grant college credit—or both—for AP scores of 4 or 5, a significant number of colleges will also recognize an AP score of 3.

Can one or more AP scores be withheld from colleges?

Yes. Students can withhold or even cancel one or more scores, but AP Services must receive the written request no later than June 15. If your child decides to withhold a score, it can still be sent later if desired. Canceled scores are permanently deleted. For details, follow this link: apscore.collegeboard.org/scores/score-reporting.

How are AP scores sent to colleges?

Scores can be sent to colleges and viewed online through this website: www.apscore.org. If you have any questions, the number for students and parents to call is 1-888-Call4AP.

How important is it to take one or more AP courses in high school?

It depends on the tier of college or university for which your child is aiming. Typically, the most competitive colleges are more likely to accept students who have enrolled in additional AP courses. Thus, it makes sense for your child to enroll in as demanding a course load as possible throughout the high-school years. AP courses are not for everyone, however, and some students might become either overwhelmed or stretched so thin that grades suffer as a result.

Is it better to perform well in a regular course as opposed to performing more poorly in an AP course?

This question comes up often. The best answer is that your child should be in the class where your child can be most successful. Colleges want students to challenge themselves in rigorous courses and do well. If your child is struggling in an AP course, your child should discuss with the teacher whether the course is the right fit. For selective colleges, student applicants are taking an array of AP courses and will need to do well in them in order to be competitive.

The High-School Transcript

Will colleges accept SAT or ACT scores listed on the high-school transcript, or do they require original copies?

Colleges generally require original copies of standardized test results. Send scores directly from the testing company. For the SAT and SAT subject tests, go to www.collegeboard.org, and for the ACT go to www.act.org. The Score Choice option allows students to submit SAT and ACT scores by test date, and SAT subject test by test. Colleges will either ask for all scores or accept the highest scores from whatever test dates your child submits, which is known as "superscoring."

If a college asks for all SAT or ACT test dates to be submitted and you're tempted to try and bypass that requirement, we urge you not to do so. Colleges can contact guidance counselors to inquire whether a student took the SAT, SAT subject test, or ACT on a particular test date. Don't try to circumvent the requirement because it can result in the student being rejected. Colleges try to give students the benefit of the doubt, and if there's a legitimate reason why a particular set of scores was below expectation, the school counselor should be informed. For example, if someone in the family just had surgery or there was a recent divorce, it would explain why a student's test scores were below par. When in doubt, either you or your child should talk with the guidance counselor, who can incorporate this relevant information in the school recommendation.

The high-school transcript/GPA weighs AP and honors courses. Will that help my child get into college?

Research has shown that high schools that weigh AP and/or honors courses appear to offer students an advantage. That said, many colleges have their own internal system of recalculating all grades from secondary schools that weigh or don't weigh grade point averages in order to level the playing field. Some of these colleges omit freshman year grades when recalculating. Other colleges may use the high-school profile for guidance. The school profile typically offers an overview of the community while providing facts and figures, including standardized test data, graduation rates, student achievement, Advanced Placement courses offered, and an overall academic synopsis.

Does senior year count for college admission?

Not only does it count, but it can also make the difference between being accepted or rejected. Most colleges will want to see your child's midyear grades, which typically include first- and second-quarter grades. The high-school transcript with senior-year final grades will be sent to the college your child plans to attend. Any significant drop in grades can have serious consequences. Those consequences typically range from a written reprimand to putting the student on probation. In extreme cases, the college might even rescind a positive admissions decision. The bottom line is that colleges expect the final transcript sent by your child's high school to reflect grades comparable to past performance. It's never too early for your child to get serious about academic performance. It's important to recognize that colleges look at trends in your child's academic program from ninth to twelfth grades.

If the student's scholastic "trajectory" is on an up-swing, it demonstrates maturity and steady progress during the high-school years. If there is a downward trend in the high-school record, it's crucial that the student reverse the trend and improve performance. If there were any personal or family issues that contributed to a downward trend, even for a single year, it's important to notify the school counselor about it. The counselor can address it in the letter of recommendation to the colleges.

My student took AP classes and got Bs, but a number of classmates took all regular classes and got As and A–s. Will my child be at a disadvantage?

No. While colleges prefer AP classes with grades in the A range, they recognize that higher-level courses are much more rigorous than the traditional high-school course. According to many college admissions officers, the degree of rigor in the courses a student has taken is a significant criterion in evaluating that individual for admission. Admissions offices usually want to see students take the most challenging courses. If a student's grades fall below a B-, however, we suggest the student talk with the school counselor and the subject teacher. Dropping down to the high school–level course, if one is offered, may be the right move. Also, many schools only allow a course to be dropped without penalty (meaning it won't appear on the high-school transcript) during a specified window of time. So when a student is choosing courses, it's important to know from the outset what the school policy is regarding dropping a course.

Does a GPA consist of only major subjects, or does it include all courses?

It depends on the individual high school. Many high schools include all courses except physical education. We suggest you or your child discuss it with the school counselor.

What is Naviance? If my school uses it, how do we use it to figure out whether my child's GPA will make my child eligible for specific schools?

Many schools use a college information system called Naviance, which has information about how your child's GPA will relate to getting into schools because of the GPA they require. Naviance will give you national data and school-specific data. Pay most attention to school-specific data, which tracks where students at your child's school were accepted based on GPA and SAT/ACT results.

What Are Colleges Looking for?

How much does a student's eleventh-grade record contribute to the application?

Considered almost universally to be the most challenging of all the high-school years, eleventh grade is when students are not only responsible for taking challenging courses, but are simultaneously preparing for standardized tests and often juggling a more independent social life. Colleges recognize that competing academic and social pressures make time and stress management, as well as honed study skills and a solid work ethic, all critical to success. So, the junior year record provides colleges with the most recent full-year indicator of how a student will perform under stressful conditions.

This isn't meant to suggest that other high-school years don't count. Colleges evaluate your child's entire secondary school transcript including academic trends, and, of course, all high-school years do contribute to the GPA (and rank, if your high-school ranks).

What do colleges look for in an applicant?

Colleges look for students who stand out. They want well-rounded individuals who have dynamic special talents or abilities. They're also looking for students who not only fit within the upper range of their high school's academic profile, but also whose background and extracurricular activities indicate that they will be active and contributing members of their college community. It's less about the quantity of activities and more about the quality of leadership and passion for their extracurricular activities.

My child took honors courses in eighth grade. Do they count in the GPA?

The high-school GPA may encompass honors and accelerated classes from eighth grade, and will certainly include all courses from ninth grade onward, possibly excluding physical education. A number of high schools also give credit for foreign language in eighth grade, depending on either the state education policy or local school district regulations.

Should my child apply to a school even if the GPA and/or standardized test scores are lower than a college's published score range?

Selecting a range of schools—taking into account safety, target, and reaches—is the way to go. Students should apply to reach schools with the understanding that while they're long shots, some of them might be looking for something that stands out other than grades and standardized test scores.

How can my child stand out to a college?

The high-school record, standardized test scores, college essays, recommendation letters, and extracurricular activities, along with the college interview (whenever recommended or required), provide an overall picture of your child as a student and as a person. Students should challenge themselves academically, do their best, prepare seriously for the SAT/ACT, and take on leadership roles in extracurricular activities. Students should re-search each school and show that they are a good fit throughout their applications. Have them do their own due diligence. Additionally, if your child has any talents, let the colleges know. If your child has had any signifi-cant experiences, or, for example, made a difference in someone's life, in the school, or in the community, don't keep it a secret. If students don't toot their own horns, no one will hear the music.

Bottom line: This is the time for your child to self-advocate. Highlight achievements both inside and out-side the classroom, and demonstrate the ways your child will add to each school's campus environment. In life, your child will need to be his or her own best advo-cate. This is the ideal time to start!

Extracurricular Activities

My child is a member of eight clubs but has never held a position of leadership in any. Is that a problem?

It's all about quality, not quantity. Being a valued member of one or more school organizations will work in your child's favor, but rising to one or more positions of leadership will significantly enhance an application. In other words, being a member of three or four clubs and having leadership roles is preferable to being a member of eight clubs and having no positions of leadership. In either case, when it comes to applying to colleges, your school counselor will be getting feedback from the faculty advisers of these clubs and can incorporate activities, contributions, commitment, and dedication in their letter of recommendation.

Is community service critical to an application?

Whenever someone offers services free of charge that benefit either the public or an institution, it's considered community service. It's often organized through the person's high school; through other organizations in the community, such as religious institutions; or through charities. Listing it on an application is not critical, but it's often helpful. Colleges generally like to see students engaged in their communities. It tells them something about character, and it suggests that the student is an active participant in the school community.

How does my child make extracurricular activities stand out to a college?

As previously stated, colleges typically view students who have been active participants in their high-school community as likely to be equally active contributors to their college community. On your child's application, begin by listing the activities and leadership roles for which your child has the greatest passion. Those ideally are also the ones your child participated in the longest. Consider having club advisers submit a statement to the school counselor highlighting contributions your child made to the organization. If the club is directly associated with a selected college major, consider having the adviser submit the letter directly to the school (e.g., if your child is a long-time member of the computer science club and is majoring in computers in college). The same holds true if the organization has been a showcase for a specific talent.

If a student doesn't have many extracurricular school activities, will that hurt the student's chances?

It might. Colleges want their students to be active members of the campus community, so they look for applicants who are engaged in their high schools. Sometimes students can't dedicate as much time as they would like to extracurricular activities because of family responsibilities, a job, or a special talent they are pursuing through private instruction. It's important to let the colleges know the situation, rather than allowing them to make assumptions.

Instead of school activities, my child plays a musical instrument for several hours every afternoon. How can we let colleges know about this?

Give them as much information as possible about your child's music and private instruction. Consider having the music teacher submit either a supplemental letter of recommendation to colleges about your child's talent or comments to your guidance counselor that can be incorporated into the school recommendation.

Athletics

My child plays on a sports team. Will that help with admissions?

That depends on a number of factors. For the committed athlete who has been playing competitively throughout many school years, the answer is an unequivocal yes. If that athlete is also a gifted player, the advantages are obvious. Conversely, if your child joins a team during junior or senior year, the impact on college applications will likely be minimal.

But what about all those students in between?

What colleges look for in terms of sports participation is commitment, ability, leadership, good sportsmanship, and a willingness to get involved in the life of the school. So if your child's involvement on a sports team would demonstrate one or more of these traits in a positive light, then yes, this aspect of school life would be an advantage in applying to college.

What role, if any, does my child's coach play in the admissions process?

Your child's coach can guide your child by helping determine if a Division I, II, or III college is the best fit. Furthermore, while it's your child's responsibility to reach out to college coaches, the high-school coach can be an effective liaison between your child and the college coaches.

Should my child's coach and school counselor be in regular contact?

Regular contact isn't necessary. Your counselor does need to get a feedback form from the coach, highlighting your child's strengths and abilities in the sport. This information will ultimately be incorporated into the college recommendation. High-school coaches are also good people to contact as motivators if you sense your child is starting to fade academically at any point, especially during senior year.

Will my child's coach contact the college coaches?

If your child is talented and demonstrates leadership abilities, and the coach is supportive, then the coach will likely reach out to the college-level counterparts. Additionally, if your child goes to the athletics section of any college website, your child should be able to get the coach's e-mail address and send the coach an introductory note about wanting to play on the team. That said, your child should continue to work with the high-school coach on everything involved in this process.

Is there anything else that is important to know?

Yes, and this is very important. If your child is applying to Division I and/or Division II schools, your child must register with the NCAA Eligibility Center during junior year. This is not necessary for Division III schools. Here are the steps to take:

a. Go to www.ncaa.org
b. Click Student-Athletes at the top of the page.
c. Access the "Guide for the College Bound Student-Athlete," which has all the information you need to know.

d. Under the same heading, go to NCAA Eligibility Center. Enter as a Student-Athlete.

e. Click on "Resources" at the top of the page and go to "Forms." Your child must print the transcript release form and give it to the counselor so the transcript can be sent. At "Resources," you have another opportunity to access the "Guide for the College Bound Student-Athlete."

f. If you want to find out which schools offer which sports, click on "Sports" at the top of the page and flip through pages 2–5.

g. It's most important that your child register for an account at the top right-hand corner, complete all the necessary questions, and get an ID number.

h. All this information should be shared with your child's counselor and coach.

Registration is extremely important because it will determine if your child has the academic profile to play Division I or II sports based on GPA in combination with SAT/ACT scores. When students register, they will need to download a transcript release form and give it to their counselor so the counselor can forward their high-school transcript and continue sending updated transcripts through the end of senior year. The Eligibility Center/Clearinghouse will list all your child's high school's course offerings and, in addition to the transcript, will need your child's SAT/ACT scores in order to evaluate and clear a student to be eligible to play. At the website, you will be able to access a guide, "The Prospective Student Athlete," and read about the rules, including the recruiting and scholarship rules for athletes.

Shouldn't my child be mostly focused on doing well in college?

Yes. In the term "Student-Athlete," your child is a student first and must choose an appropriate school in order to be a successful student and balance both academics and athletics. Your child must meet with college coaches to see what kind of tutoring and support services are given to student athletes and, at the end of the day, must choose a college that is the best fit and at which your child can be most successful. Many student athletes are recruited by selective schools because they are so athletically talented, but the academics of the schools are way too difficult.

The Performing and Visual Arts Student

My child is interested in studying one of the performing or visual arts (art, drama, musical theatre, music performance, or dance). Where do we start?

A good starting place is the National Association of College Admissions Counselors website. In addition to "Tips for the Performing and Visual Arts Student," there is information about Performing Arts College Fairs around the country, where schools with these programs will be represented. You and your child will be able to speak with representatives at colleges that offer these specific programs and pick up informational brochures.

    a. Go to http://nacacnet.org.
    b. Click "College Fairs" at the top of the page.
    c. Click "Performing and Visual Arts Fair Schedule."
    d. On the right side of the page you will see fair schedules, how to get started, and tips you and your child need to know.

How will this route affect the college process?

In addition to the application for admission, there will be auditions (for music, dance, and theatre students) as well as portfolio requirements for art students. These requirements and procedures for fulfilling them will be listed on the college website.

Does this involve more deadlines, supplements, and layers to the whole process?

Yes, and sometimes it can get demanding. Your child will need to arrange for preauditions/auditions, portfolio review, and so forth, and this can involve an additional section of the application.

How will my child know how to submit supplemental materials such as an art portfolio or a YouTube video of acting, singing, dancing, and so on?

When your child fills out the application and checks off the desired program, there will be information about this process. Many colleges ask students to use Slideroom to submit these materials.

What is Slideroom?

Slideroom (http://www.slideroom.com) partners with the Common Application so students can send media within the application process. When your child applies to a particular school for an arts program, your child may be directed to Slideroom to submit the required materials.

I want my child to have opportunities outside the arts just in case my child doesn't become a famous actor, musician, dancer, or singer. How can we make sure that other schools are chosen that have other opportunities?

Some schools are totally focused on a specific arts area: music conservatories and art schools have few opportunities for study outside the student's chosen area of focus. Other schools and universities may have a school of music or a school of visual arts within the larger university setting. Attending such a school will give a student more opportunities to study other disciplines, while also maintaining a study of the arts.

I heard that if a student is talented but is not such a great student, their talent will get them into college. Is this true?

At many schools, students are not only evaluated for talent but also evaluated on their academic performance. Thus, both are important factors in the admissions process. Conservatories and art schools, of course, are looking mainly at talent. Some schools will allow students to submit proof of their creative talent, though they may not want to major in that area, and schools will use this additional information in the admissions process, which can help students.

My child works with a private music teacher, gets private art or singing lessons, and/or is involved in the school drama program, art program, and so on. Should we bounce things off these instructors and faculty advisers?

Absolutely—bring everybody into the discussion to assess your child's ability in an effort to move forward realistically. These people can be great resources in addition to the school counselor.

Will my child need a separate résumé that highlights all experiences in my child's chosen area of interest?

It is a good idea to develop this type of résumé to send with application materials. Upload it as a supplement to your child's application and bring it to interviews, auditions, and portfolio reviews.

Summer Activities

How important are summer activities to colleges?

Summer activities provide a snapshot to colleges about how your child spends free time. Is your child reading, traveling, doing community service, taking an enrichment or college-level course, or working? Or does summer mean loafing around, doing nothing but sleeping late, going on Facebook, hanging out, tweeting, playing video games, and texting? There is a difference.

My child did nothing last summer except sleep late and have fun. Will that hurt an application?

If a college likes your child's overall credentials, then summer activities won't likely be a factor in admission. When it comes to reach schools, however, every little bit of insurance matters. For example, imagine there are ten remaining slots to be filled in a freshman class, and there are twenty applicants. Assuming the applicants all have similar credentials, but ten had productive summers and the others lounged around, guess who would have the edge?

How can I find out about different summer opportunities for my child?

Check with your child's school counselor and check your child's school's website at the guidance section. Guidance offices receive tons of mail about summer programs and may inform students and parents about them in different ways. There is nothing wrong with getting a summer job to save money for college and to develop responsible working skills. Colleges truly respect this choice. If your child is interested in a specific college, check the college's website for "Summer Programs for High School Students." Spending a couple of weeks on a college campus, one that interests your child, is a great way to experience the campus, the classes, and the college environment. Be aware that some of these programs are expensive, and applications need to be in as early as January of senior year.

My child likes to travel. Will that help an application?

It might. If it involves occasional traveling with family or friends, that likely won't make a difference. If the travel is purposeful or enriching, though, it could certainly make for a more interesting and possibly stronger application. For example, if your child traveled to a third world country and helped build homes or plant crops, it would be a plus. Or perhaps the travel could be tied in to an academic strength or career dream. If your child took college-level courses in another country, that, too, would be advantageous.

Should we ask for a letter from an employer, camp counselor, or supervisor to give to the school counselor?

Any positive learning experience your child has should conclude with a request for a recommendation letter at the end of the summer. The mentor (camp counselor, teacher, professor, coach, supervisor, etc.) should write a recommendation and send it to your child's school counselor. This will provide the counselor with another useful perspective, broadening and enriching the college letter of recommendation.

What is one major activity that all rising seniors must do in the summer before senior year?

The Common Application, used by most colleges, goes live on August 1. Your child should register for an account on August 1 and work on completing the Common Application before school officially begins. Many school's supplements may not be available until the fall, but your child can complete the core of the application. Essay questions are usually released in March.

Interview and College Visits

Does a college interview help my child's chances of being accepted?

While some college interviews will become a part of the admissions process, they usually only highlight things that are already listed in the application. In the interview, colleges hope to learn more about the kind of student your child would be in class, in the dorms, and in campus life. If an interview is neither required nor recommended, or if it's a group interview, then it's not going to be a factor in the admissions decision.

If there were any unusual circumstances during high school, such as a divorce or death of someone in your family, and it had an impact on your child's grades, an informal interview might be helpful in conveying the specific circumstances. Having a college interview can certainly help a student's chances if it's required or recommended. If that's the case, we suggest that your child prepare for the interview in advance with either the guidance counselor or with a private college adviser.

What should my child wear to a college interview, and what is the best way to prepare?

The college interview can help bring an application to life, but you should remember that it won't weigh too heavily on the admission decision. That being said, we would suggest dressing casually and neatly. It's not a black-tie event, but students should wear appropriate attire.

To prepare, consider doing some role-playing situations with the guidance counselor; practice does help. Your child should prepare one or two thoughtful questions to ask your interviewer. Bring a student copy of their high-school transcript in case the interviewer would like to refer to it; this shows good foresight on your child's part. Your child may also bring a résumé. Be certain cell phones are turned off and kept out of sight.

If, during the interview, your child is asked a question that is totally unexpected, your child should not attempt to rush a response. It's okay to pause or say, "Let me think about that for a moment." Another good way to handle this is to rephrase the interviewer's question and ask if the question was correctly understood. It may prompt the interviewer to give your child a bit more of a lead about what they're looking for.

What sort of questions should a student prepare to ask at the interview?

Students should prepare a few questions that will demonstrate serious research about this college. Avoid questions that could have been easily answered by browsing the college's website or in the literature the student read about academics, campus life, clubs, and community-service opportunities. Students can ask about safety on campus, about the college's retention rate, or even about career advisement for students entering senior year. Questions should not suggest that your student knows little about the college. For example, don't ask if the college offers a major in biology or if the dorms are coed. Your child might even want to ask about the interviewer's favorite feature/aspect/opportunity of campus life.

Is it appropriate to use a college interview as an opportunity to explain some special circumstances that affected a student's high-school performance?

Yes, it's appropriate to use this opportunity to discuss any potential red flags on a student's transcript, but be honest. Your child doesn't want a lie to come back and bite. For example, if asked why grades slipped freshman year, it's okay to tell the interviewer about a divorce or an illness. If, on the other hand, the real reason grades were lower than they should have been was because of friends, relationships, or other distractions, students might want to acknowledge the missteps but say that they have done a lot of growing up and now have their priorities in order, as demonstrated in recent academic reports. They should always think beforehand about any possible negatives, and discuss them with school counselors and family members first. The counselor's letter of recommendation will complement your child's honest comments in a way that will be beneficial.

What are the magic words that will make my child the one they choose?

There are no magic words, unfortunately. But there are some powerful ways that your child can increase the chances of standing out. Know the college well enough to prepare intelligent questions to ask during the interview. Go into the interview with a confident mind-set and greet the interviewer with a smile, making direct eye contact and offering a solid handshake. During the interview, maintain good eye contact and thank the interviewer for the time and attention provided. Then follow up by sending a thank-you note. Attention to these small but important details makes a strong and favorable impression. Everything your child says and does tells the college something. This can help differentiate applicants who may be similar in a number of other categories.

Is an alumni interview as good as an on-campus interview?

It's fine, but don't use it as a substitute for visiting the college, if circumstances permit. Colleges generally keep track of who comes to visit through campus tours and on-site interviews.

If your child applies somewhere Early Action, it can be advantageous to visit that college in advance. If your child applies Early Decision, however, it is imperative to visit that college before making a binding commitment. If making it to the college in person is not possible, try to ensure your child makes an effort to demonstrate interest beyond passively looking at the college website or quietly sitting in the back of high-school information sessions.

A representative from a college my child is interested in attending is coming to the high school to talk with students. Is there anything my child should do or ask?

During the meeting, your child should listen intently (no distractions), get any handouts or brochures offered, and take notes. After the conference, suggest that your child ask for the representative's business card, which will have contact information on it, and ask for permission to call or e-mail with any further questions. Be sure that you remind your child to say thank you and shake hands before leaving and send a follow-up e-mail soon after the session, telling the representative some specific things about the college that were particularly attractive or intriguing.

My child was not asked to have an alumni interview. Does that mean my child is not being considered for admission?

No. Sometimes colleges just don't have the time or resources to meet with everyone. Just make sure your child keeps working hard! It will not affect your child's application in any way.

My child had an interview (either on-campus or alumni), and it only lasted twenty minutes. Does that mean the college is no longer interested?

Not at all. Interviews can range in time from fifteen minutes to over an hour.

Should a thank-you e-mail be sent after attending interviews and information sessions?

It's highly recommended to do so. A thank-you note demonstrates maturity and will further differentiate your child from other applicants. It will take five minutes to send a message of appreciation to the interviewer. It can't hurt, it just might help, and it's simply the right thing to do.

When should students sign up to visit college campuses?

The best time is in the spring of junior year. That's when the regular student body is present, and students will get to see campus life firsthand. While it's more convenient to visit during the summer, your child won't get a feel for the social atmosphere of the campus in full swing. If they are too busy during the school year, visit colleges in late August or early September and then revisit the one or two that were top choices later on.

What else should students do besides take an organized tour?

Talk to students on campus, check out the college bookstore, visit the admissions office, and eat in the students' dining hall. If the college either requires or recommends an interview, schedule it in advance for that same day. Also, get a copy of the school's newspaper and go to open houses. Your child should bring a pen and paper and take notes about impressions, both positive and negative, because once you start visiting colleges, details do become hazy. If your child is interested in a particular academic area, it's a good idea to make an appointment to speak with someone in the department. After the visit, if your child likes the school, your child should sign up to be on the school's mailing/e-mail list. This can be done on the college website.

Can my child sit in on classes? Stay overnight?

Your child can stay overnight with a friend, and, if a professor permits it, attend one or more classes (this should be arranged in advance). Ask the high-school counselor if there's a contact list of any recent graduates who are willing to talk with, meet with, or offer housing to prospective students.

Should my child arrange to speak with anyone in particular on campus?

If your child met anyone from the college who previously visited the high school, all efforts should be made to see that person. E-mail the college representative in advance to be sure the person is available on the day of your child's visit. If the representative is out of town when you visit the campus, see if your child can meet with someone else in the admissions office. We also encourage striking up informal conversations with students on campus, particularly students in the cafeteria, in the library, or in the halls of classrooms specific to your child's interests (e.g., in the labs if your child loves science), gleaning valuable student perspectives about each college.

The College Essay

What is the college essay used for?

It gives the colleges a chance to learn more about your child's personality, writing style, priorities, and beliefs. It's important that a family member and an English teacher review what your child writes and offer recommendations. Your school counselor can also be a reader. A well-written, insightful essay can make a huge difference.

My child is having trouble selecting a topic for the personal statement. Any suggestions?

Begin by looking through the activities list, community service or paid work efforts, and other life-altering or meaningful experiences. Try to find a defining incident, significant accomplishment, "Aha" moment, or an outstanding aspect of a particular "story" that can be captured in an engaging essay. The essay gives the admissions officers a memorable perspective on applicants and helps them stand out among hundreds of other students.

Who should my child ask to proofread their college essay?

Colleges expect students to submit a polished essay. Therefore, it is valuable to have some objective readers take a look at the essay before submitting it. Students can reach out to mentors such as a guidance counselor or English teacher. Parents can also help proofread and give suggestions.

How important is the college essay?

The college essay is one of the most important determining factors in the admission process. It brings a student's voice to the application, creating the best opportunity to share views and experiences with admissions officers. It is essential that your child write self-reflective essays that both provoke thought and engage interest. It's also important to respect the suggested word counts and strive to be on-point and succinct.

Are there any off-limits topics?

Nothing is off-limits, but common sense should dictate your child's choice of subject matter. If your child is thinking about sharing any controversial topic, run it by both family members and the guidance counselor in advance.

Can students exceed the word limit?

Admissions offices like applicants who don't go over the word count. Online applications such as the Common Application typically don't allow that; the essay will be cut off once the word limit has been reached. Much more than twenty-five words beyond what's expected is more likely to hurt rather than help, though many schools do not mind as long as the additional text is within reason and directly helpful in portraying the applicant. On the Common Application, there is a minimum requirement of 250 words and a maximum limit of 650 words for the personal statement.

Supplemental essays vary in length by school and topic, so your child should try to stay within the limits while using as much real estate as possible to make the application stand out.

Letters of Recommendation

How many letters of recommendation do students need from teachers?

Colleges typically require the school counselor letter of recommendation as well as the School Report along with either one or two teacher recommendations. Your child can submit an additional letter or two, but they should come from individuals with a different perspective, such as a coach, school principal, or other significant person in a student's life. Sending more recommendations does not increase your chance of being admitted, so most admissions officers prefer you to stick within their recommendation guidelines.

Which teachers should students ask to write college recommendations?

Your child should try to elicit recommendations from the teachers of your child's strongest subjects that reflect the choice of college major (if already known). For example, if your child wants to major in journalism, consider asking an eleventh-grade English teacher; an accounting major might ask an eleventh-grade math teacher. In general, colleges want recommendations to be written by eleventh-grade teachers, preferably a math/science teacher and an English/social studies/foreign-language teacher. Sometimes a letter of recommendation from a teacher of a class in which your child did not do as well can be the best letter. If the student struggled, worked hard, and met with the teacher continuously for extra help, the teacher can elaborate on the student's strong work ethic in a challenging class. Colleges will see that the student is persevering and will use all the resources of the college to succeed.

We agree with the trend at colleges such as Yale and SUNY Binghamton that recommend students ask for reference letters from teachers who know them best, with whom there has been a sustained relationship, and who can reflect on your child's work ethic. While eleventh-grade teachers are excellent candidates to write recommendation letters, they should not exclude a tenth-grade teacher who may know your child better, and who has maintained a relationship through extra-curricular activities or community service.

My guidance counselor really doesn't know my child well. Will that hurt my child's chances?

Probably not. Your child's guidance counselor uses a number of resources to write letters of recommendation, including a student's guidance records, high-school transcript, standardized test scores, and feedback from teachers, such as anecdotes that your child might be encouraged to gather. Parents and students can give counselors insight about students' greatest strengths, most outstanding accomplishments, and circumstances that may have impacted their educational or personal experience. Keep in mind as well that it's never too late for your child to make an appointment with the guidance counselor to provide new information and share concerns, or just to get to know the counselor better.

Should students waive their right to read teacher recommendations?

Definitely. Waiving the right to read teacher recommendations signals to colleges that whatever teachers and counselors write about your child will be an honest evaluation of high-school performance. Not signing the waiver is a red flag and typically results in a reference letter that is less than candid, which colleges would find suspect. Signing the waiver significantly increases the value of the submitted recommendations, which, in turn, enhances your child's credentials.

I'm worried that a teacher might write a bad recommendation about my child.

Teachers are not looking to hurt students. If your child approaches a teacher about a letter of recommendation for college and receives an enthusiastic yes, trust the educator. Writing a recommendation takes a lot of time and effort, so professionals aren't going to waste their time writing a letter that's going to hurt your son or daughter. At the same time, if your child asks an instructor to write a letter and the instructor makes an excuse such as, "I'm too busy now" or questions whether they're the best person to ask, your child should take the hint and ask another teacher.

Our priest/rabbi has known my child for many years. Should a religious figure be asked to write a recommendation? Should we send in supplemental letters of recommendation from a coach or employer?

Supplemental letters that share useful information about your child are always welcome, as long as an applicant doesn't go overboard and send too many. Your child can either have these individuals submit letters directly to the colleges, or ask them to send their comments to a guidance counselor, who can incorporate that information into the school recommendation. Generally, having your child's counselor include such comments in a school recommendation works best.

Feedback Forms to Share with the Guidance Counselor

What is a "feedback form"?

A feedback form provides the school counselor with relevant and useful information about your child from people who know your child well, based on significant interactions, whether in the classroom, on the athletic field, or through an important extracurricular activity in or out of school. This form, often called "an anecdotal," is used solely by your child's school counselor and is never sent to any colleges. It can, however, provide invaluable insights to your child's guidance counselor when preparing the letter of recommendation. These feedback forms differ from the official letters of recommendation that teachers send directly to colleges either by mail or electronically through software programs such as Naviance.

Why is a feedback form helpful?

The school counselor typically knows your child through the guidance file, group sessions, and individual counselor meetings. The feedback forms provide the counselor with the voices of others who know your child from different perspectives, permitting a much more enriched perception of your child, and allowing the counselor to write a more thorough and nuanced recommendation. Remembering to distribute these forms is an important and strategic step that will be clearly beneficial.

How do I know that teachers will only write positive things about my child?

You don't, which is why your child should choose carefully (e.g., Which teachers know me best? Where have I had the most positive experiences?). Even if a teacher submits a less-than-glowing form, the counselor is under no obligation to include that in the letter of recommendation.

Your child's counselor will review all of the gathered information, and ultimately will use discretion to best represent your child to the colleges.

What about feedback from someone other than my child's teachers?

The feedback forms can be given to anyone who knows your child well. A coach; an extracurricular-activities adviser; a religious figure in your church, synagogue, or mosque; an employer; or a family member—any of these could offer a unique perspective of your child that would add an important dimension about the student.

Should anyone in our family submit a feedback form for my child?

Absolutely. You know your child better than anyone, and can address what you view as your child's greatest achievements, list adjectives, highlight strengths, describe any circumstances that may have impacted your child's performance or well-being in school, and anything else you feel is pertinent. We also recommend that your child complete a self-reflection feedback form, answering some or all of the same questions asked of you. In addition, your child can highlight any particular talents and significant school or community activities, sharing why these aspects hold such importance. This is your child's chance to shine. The more information the school counselor has about your child, the better.

My child's school doesn't offer feedback forms. What should we do?

Even if your child's school does not offer feedback forms, there's no reason why you and your child cannot go ahead and submit your own written comments to share with the school counselor. Additionally, have your child ask favorite teachers to write a short blurb and submit it to the counselor.

My child has a job. Should my child give a feedback form to an employer?

If your child has worked at a particular job on a regular basis and is close with the supervisor, then a feedback form from that individual would be helpful to show work ethic and job performance. Employers can either give the student's counselor a feedback form or write a blurb. Either way, check with the college to find out whether the recommendation should be mailed to your child's school counselor or to the college directly.

Should my child give a feedback form to a teacher from this current year?

It depends. If your child is applying to one or more colleges Early Decision (ED) or Early Action (EA), there's little time for a teacher to truly get to know the student. The school counselor should not be held up on sending a recommendation while waiting for the teacher's feedback form. If your child previously had the same teacher and had a good experience, though, then it could be considered. Also, if your child is not applying either ED or EA, then there may be enough time for a current teacher to develop a constructive relationship with your child in order to write a helpful recommendation.

Social-Media Smarts

Do we need to worry about a college searching for students on social-media networks?

In a word—absolutely! Admissions officers do not always look for students on social-media networks, but that doesn't mean students shouldn't present themselves well online. Online scrutiny of college applicants is growing, and a student's digital footprint can play a significant role in the admissions process.

What your child shares online may be viewable by many—those "privacy settings" have to be closely monitored! So assume all these people may be looking online to gather additional information about your child's character and activities: college admissions officers, scholarship coordinators, financial aid officers, athletic recruiters, teachers who are writing recommendations, potential employers for internships and jobs, and assorted other organizations.

What precautions should my child take to make sure the online image my child has on all social-media accounts (including Facebook, Google, YouTube, Pinterest, Twitter, Tumblr, Vine, Instagram, and Foursquare) will be as appropriate and free of potentially damaging material as possible?

Your child should review ALL social-media profiles, as there may be some that are linked to one another. A privacy setting enables the user to determine who is allowed to view all postings, photos, tags, and "likes." Regularly monitoring these settings enables the student to remain in control of what others can see. Remind your child to be certain that there are no inappropriate posts or photos dating back to when an account was opened with each particular social-media site.

Photos of the student drinking alcohol (or any illegal activity), being in the company of others who are engaging in these activities, using rude or profane language or gestures, or participating in any sexual or sexually sug-gestive activities are the sort of incriminating posts and pictures your child should delete immediately.

Encourage your child to check for any "tags" and pages that may have been "liked" that could be compro-mising or embarrassing. This may seem less obvious, but providing private contact information such as a phone number or address demonstrates poor judgment, and even the username and handles that your child chooses to use are revelatory to an astute observer. So a simple, direct username and a professional profile with a digni-fied photo will make an appropriate statement. At the same time, your child should be proactive in cultivat-ing a positive profile on social-media sites. The groups students join, the pages they "like," and the posts they make can provide a view into interesting and unexpect-ed dimensions of students' lives.

Finally, admissions officers (and others like potential employers) are technology savvy and well aware that students maintain two Facebook accounts. In short, keep them wholesome!

Senior Year: The Fall Semester

How important is the fall semester? Why does it count as heavily as the junior year?

Colleges place significance on the junior year and the fall semester of senior year. The fall semester of senior year provides colleges with the most up-to-date information about your child's scholastic performance in what is typically the most academically rigorous curriculum of a high-school career. Juniors balance an increasingly demanding course load with extracurricular activities while also devoting hours to prepare for and then take multiple standardized tests, and colleges believe they are learning to handle the level of pressure that undergraduate studies will demand. Those students who continue to excel during these school years impress colleges as good candidates for admission.

What if my child doesn't do well in the first quarter of senior year?

The student must identify the source of difficulty and rectify the situation as quickly as possible. If your child is considering dropping a course, look up the deadline to ensure the course won't appear as "withdrawn" on the transcript. If there's any doubt, speak to the school counselor as soon as possible.

Should we send first-quarter grades to colleges that my child applied to Early Decision or Early Action?

Yes, especially if they represent a steadiness of grades from prior years and certainly if they demonstrate a positive upturn in grades. In either case, your child may want to talk with the guidance counselor before making a final decision.

My child did very well in four out of five academic courses. Should we still send first-quarter grades?

This depends on which course was weakest, the grade, and previous grades in that subject. In general, as long as grades, especially in academic subjects, are at least as good as or better than in prior years, we recommend sending them.

The Wait list

Do students get accepted from the waitlist?

The waitlist is designed to inform applicants that colleges are serious about them; otherwise, the student would have received a letter of denial. When colleges hear back from admitted students regarding the acceptance of their offers, spots will open up on the waitlist. At that point, colleges will contact those students whom they placed on the waitlist, offering some of them admission.

Is there anything a student can do to improve the chance of being accepted from the waitlist?

Certainly. In the body of an e-mail (not as an attachment) to the Office of Undergraduate Admissions, copying the local recruiter, the student must state the tidbits of information that are relevant since submission of the original application:

1. Acknowledge that the student has been deferred or waitlisted.
2. State that the school remains the student's first choice (colleges love to admit students when they know it is the student's dream school).
3. Promise to attend if admitted (if this REALLY is the case).
4. Update any information (e.g., honors, awards, contests, competitions, scholarships, publications, jobs, community-service endeavors, tutoring, new athletic, musical or artistic developments, club activities, visits to the college campus, meeting with professors, securing a summer job, and commencement speaker).
5. Send first- and second-semester grades, and state that the student has remained steadfast and academically focused while juggling a more demanding course load, remaining an active participant in both the school and community, and preparing for standardized tests.
6. Send significant standardized test score increases.

7. Reiterate the student's hope that this new information will help convince the school to admit the student to the class of_____.

8. Give an in-depth focus on the most impressive new qualification in detail, emphasizing how this achievement will help make a positive contribution to the college. Do some additional research on the college and discuss how the student envisions life on campus. Be specific about the courses, professors, and clubs that the student is most excited about.

9. Request that this e-mail update be included in the student's admission application folder. State that the student is hoping for good news.

10. Remember to include full name, address, cell number, e-mail address, ID number, and date of birth.

11. Follow up the e-mail with a phone call to ensure that the admissions office has received the e-mail, and that it has been added to the student's application folder.

12. Even if your child has already visited the school, if it is among the student's first-choice schools, visit again. Putting a face to a name and an application demonstrates genuine interest. While there, your child can then restate goals and enthusiastically

discuss the contributions to the campus your child is eager to make. Arrange another visit to the school, attend classes, and meet with a professor in an area of interest. In a follow-up e-mail, be sure to mention the specific details of your additional visit along with sincere thanks.

Do we have to put a deposit at another school while we wait to see if my child gets accepted from the waitlist?

Because there is no guarantee that the student will ultimately be accepted, and may even find out just prior to the start of classes in the fall, it is critical that the student seriously consider another school. Most schools require a commitment by May 1, along with a deposit. In fact, some schools require a dorm commitment prior to May 1. Therefore, you must place a deposit at another school.

My child was admitted from the waitlist. Can I get my deposit back from the other colleges?

Not likely, since most deposits are nonrefundable. But there's no harm in calling the Office of Undergraduate Admissions to inquire.

IB Diploma

What is an IB Diploma Programme?

The IB Diploma Programme is an academically challenging, intercultural course of study intended to prepare students not only for college but also for life after their college career. It takes a holistic approach, addressing the intellectual, social, emotional, ethical, and physical aspects of the student's life in preparation for higher education and "real world" situations.

Can it help my child's chances for getting into college?

The IB offers a rigorous program of study that is considered comparable to Advanced Placement coursework among the more than two thousand colleges and universities worldwide that recognize the diploma. Just as in Advanced Placement courses, it's important to maintain strong grades.

Achieving excellent grades in this program—as in any program—will be advantageous to your child when applying to colleges. If your child is an IB candidate, it is best to contact colleges to confirm the university's policy on students with IB diplomas and whether the diploma is recognized.

Does a student with an IB diploma look better than a student enrolled in AP courses?

It depends. Students who plan to earn a traditional high-school diploma can choose the number and type of Advanced Placement courses in which they wish to enroll. Students in IB programs have a mandatory set of core re-quirements, including community service, an extended four-thousand-word essay/research paper, and six interdis-ciplinary courses. The interdisciplinary curriculum, which provides the student with a broad depth of knowledge, comes from the following disciplines: Studies in Language and Literature; Language Acquisition; Individuals and Societies; sciences, mathematics, and the arts.

Another core requirement is the TOK (theory of knowledge). Additional information can be found at www.ibo.org/diploma/curriculum/core/knowledge.

In addition, IB candidates must pass IB exams just as students in the AP program will take AP exams. Visit www.ibo.org/diploma and www.ibo.org/diploma/curriculum for additional information.

Do all colleges accept an IB degree?

While over two thousand institutions worldwide recognize the IB Diploma Programme, not every university will accept IB credits. Thus, we recommend contacting any college your child is thinking of applying to in advance to check out policies regarding IB diplomas. For a link to colleges and universities in the United States that recognize the IB diploma as of the time of this publication, check www.ibo.org/country/US/index.cfm for further information.

Do colleges prefer an IB diploma or a regular high-school diploma?

Colleges and universities that recognize the IB diploma will view it as comparable to a diploma featuring a traditional AP program. Since the IB degree requires a mandated curriculum, though, and the AP program does not, students in the traditional high-school diploma program must choose to enroll in the most rigorous academic courses available. In addition, they need to participate in extracurricular activities that facilitate their emotional and social well-being, and they must be contributing members of their high-school community.

Students with Disabilities

If my child has either an IEP or Section 504 plan, should it be shared with colleges?

You should share this information if your child is going to need accommodations or services related to the disability. The timing will depend on the particular college your child is applying to and the nature of the support you are seeking. Colleges with comprehensive or structured programs often have a separate admissions process and will want to see documentation of your child's disability early. If it's just basic services such as testing accommodations that are needed, there's no need to disclose the disability until after admission. Be sure to research the individual schools and programs and follow their instructions.

Will my child's learning differences affect admission?

No. Your child is protected under Section 504 of the Rehabilitation Act of 1973 and the Americans with Disabilities Act (ADA). These are federal civil rights statutes that prohibit discrimination against otherwise qualified individuals—people who meet the usual academic standards required for admission to a particular college. These laws mean that colleges may not place quotas on the number of students with disabilities they accept, and they may not require students to disclose their disabilities. The laws also require colleges to provide reasonable accommodations. (See question "Do all colleges provide services for students with disabilities?")

Sometimes, it can actually be beneficial to share information about your child's disability because it may help explain certain aspects of a transcript (e.g., no foreign language) and demonstrate a determination and ability to overcome obstacles.

Does my child first have to be accepted into the university in order to be accepted into a comprehensive or structured program?

It depends on the school. Each college sets its own admissions standards. Generally, your child will need to be admitted to the college before being considered for comprehensive services. But there are instances where the regular admissions office and the support program make admissions decisions in consultation with one another.

Do all colleges provide services for students with disabilities?

Section 504 and the ADA require all colleges to provide reasonable accommodations in the areas of program, instruction, and testing to ensure that they do not discriminate against students with disabilities. Requested accommodations must be directly linked to the student's disability through documentation. Colleges must provide access; they do not have to ensure success. Colleges have considerable latitude in what is reasonable. Examples of accommodations that are provided by most colleges include: reduced course load, audiobooks, note-takers, and extended time on tests. It is important to gather as much information as possible about each school under consideration to be sure your child's specific needs will be met.

What are the differences between colleges that offer comprehensive programs and those that offer only basic services?

College support programs run the gamut. Virtually all colleges offer at least basic services, including testing accommodations and generic supports such as writing centers and peer tutoring. In colleges with basic services, the contact person wears many hats and may not have any specialized training. Generally, the student discloses a disability upon admission, not before. An increasing number of colleges have begun to offer comprehensive programs, which provide significantly more support. Individual tutorial assistance with specialists, frequent monitoring of student progress, special advisement, and early registration are some of the enhanced services supervised by a full-time coordinator with expertise in learning disabilities and ADHD.

Comprehensive programs typically have a separate application process and often carry a substantial additional cost. Students are advised to apply early because there may be limited slots.

What type of documentation of my child's disability is required?

Schools vary widely in how they handle the application process for students with special needs. Check the college's website by searching for "Disability Services." Many schools will outline specific documentation that is required. Schools with comprehensive programs usually require a separate application and essay, and often a letter of recommendation from your child's resource room teacher. At the minimum, colleges will want to see the most recent IEP or 504 plan and documentation of disability in the form of a psycho-educational evaluation. Students with ADHD may be asked for a diagnostic statement from a medical professional. Before your child submits a regular application, find out exactly what documentation is required by each school. Also, ask to whom it should be mailed and when. Your child's guidance counselor and resource room teacher will be able to help fulfill all documentation requirements.

How do we know which kind of program my child will need?

In considering what kind of program your child will need in college, think about the supports utilized during the last two years of high school. If your child is still dependent on direct, regular academic assistance or receives some instruction in special-education classes, it is a safe bet that a comprehensive program in college will be necessary. If your child is independent of nearly all supports by the end of high school, then the more basic services at a college will probably suffice. Another factor to weigh is how academically challenging the college itself is—the more competitive the school, the more help your child will likely require to be successful. If you're looking at schools with comprehensive programs, meeting with representatives of these programs is just as important as any other component of the college visits. In fact, if your child will need any level of services, you should include a visit to the disabilities office when visiting a school. Call ahead to make an appointment.

Should one of the letters of recommendation for college come from my child's resource room teacher?

If your child is applying to colleges with comprehensive programs, it makes sense to have a resource room teacher write a letter, especially if that teacher has come to know your child well and the two share a good relationship. If your child is only in need of basic services, then the resource room teacher could provide an extra reference letter or offer feedback to the school counselor to include in the college letter of recommendation. In either case, a letter from a resource room teacher should supplement, not replace, letters from mainstream classroom teachers.

A disability prevented my child from taking a foreign language. Will that hurt chances for admission?

Again, the answer is, "It depends." Some colleges require students to have taken at least two years of a foreign language in high school, while others will be more open to a student who has not studied a foreign language, particularly with an explanation such as a learning disability. For certain majors, though, even the most flexible colleges absolutely require some foreign language credit. It's important to check with the colleges your child is applying to beforehand to determine whether the school has any foreign language requirement.

My child took the SAT with extended time. Will colleges know?

There is no indication on the score report, so colleges will not know unless your child chooses to tell them.

My child has a Section 504 plan, and I don't want the colleges to know about it. Is it possible to keep that confidential?

Yes, it is your child's decision whether to share this information. Your child's high school cannot share it without a special release, and colleges cannot require disclosure.

Financial Aid

What is financial aid?

Financial aid is supplemental financial support to help you pay for college. You can use your financial aid to pay for both direct costs, such as tuition, fees, and room and board, and indirect costs like books, travel, supplies, and personal expenses related to college attendance. Financial aid includes grants, scholarships, loans, and work study.

How do we apply for financial aid?

Every student regardless of family income should fill out the FAFSA, the Free Application for Federal Student Aid. The FAFSA will determine your eligibility for federal student aid, such as PELL grants, federal direct loans, and federal work study. It will also help the college determine your financial need in order to attend their institution. You complete the FAFSA online at www.fafsa.ed.gov and will have to update the FAFSA for each year that your child is attending college.

When do we apply?

You can complete the FAFSA on or after October 1. The priority deadline for first-time college students is between January 15 and February 15 for most schools. Due to another change in the FAFSA rules, families can now complete the application using their tax information from two years before the filing date. In addition, you can use the IRS Data Retrieval Tool, which links directly to the IRS to upload tax information within three weeks of electronic filing. For the CSS Profile, you should register at least two weeks before the earliest college priority deadline.

But what if I don't have my taxes done in time to get the form submitted by February 15?

No problem. It is better to do a good close estimate of your financial information and get the application in early than it is to wait until your taxes are done. The key is to do a close estimate.

You can either look at the prior year's taxes and use those as estimates, or you can use the information on the last paystubs from the previous year or from your W2 forms. Once you do your taxes, you simply log in to the FAFSA website and update your information. If your estimates were close, it should not dramatically impact your financial aid awards.

What is TAP? (New York State residents only)

TAP is the Tuition Assistance Program, a state-based grant program for New York residents who attend college within the state and demonstrate need. Students with a family income of $80,000 or below are eligible for TAP. Once you complete the FAFSA, a link to TAP will be provided after submission. Or you could go to www.tap.hesc.ny.gov. Your TAP application will be prefilled based on the information that you provided on the FAFSA. TAP will only list the first New York state college listed on your FAFSA. After you accept your admissions, you can log into your TAP application to change the school.

My child is applying for financial aid, but some of my friends' children who are applying to many of the same colleges as my child aren't asking for aid. Will this hurt my child's chances for being admitted?

The vast majority of colleges and universities are "need-blind" in their admissions process. This means that the issue of whether a student has financial need does not factor into the college's decision to admit or deny a student. As a matter of fact, the office of admissions and office of financial aid are two separate entities. Each one functions independently of the other. Each student is reviewed individually based on the particular admissions criteria of the college or university, and a person requiring financial assistance and one who does not are at an equal advantage in the process. If a university does use need as one of its admissions criteria, it is required to share that information with the applicant.

What is the FAFSA form?

The Free Application for Federal Student Aid is an application created by the federal government to gather critical information about a student's income, assets, and, where appropriate, parental income and assets for use in the determination of an estimated family contribution (EFC). The EFC isn't the minimum amount that a student has to pay; it's not the maximum amount that the student has to pay, either. As a matter of fact, the student doesn't need to pay it at all. It's just the minimum amount that the federal government says the student can contribute toward education costs. Each of the colleges that the student lists on the FAFSA form receives this information and uses the EFC to determine what type of financial aid will be offered to the student. The vast majority of colleges and universities require this FAFSA form in order for a student to be considered for any type of federal, state, or institutional aid. It's actually a pretty user-friendly form, with drop-down boxes next to each question explaining in more detail what is being requested and where to find it. The form can be found at www.fafsa.gov and remember, it's FREE!

What do I need to complete the FAFSA?

Before completing the FAFSA you will first have to register for a PIN. Your PIN will be used as your electronic signature to submit the FAFSA online. Both you and your child will need a PIN. Only one parent needs to register for a PIN, and it can be the same as the student's. To apply, you can go to www.pin.ed.gov. To register, you need your name, date of birth, and Social Security number. To complete the FAFSA you should collect the following documents: your driver's license, alien registration number (if applicable), and financial documents for those reporting income. Financial documents include: W2s, federal income tax forms, untaxed income records (Social Security, veterans' benefits, Temporary Assistance for Families), most recent bank statement, and most recent business and investment information.

What is considered a "business" for the FAFSA?

The FAFSA identifies a business as having one hundred employees or more. If your family's business has fewer than one hundred employees, then you enter "0" for the business income.

Whose income should be reported on the FAFSA?

Both the student's and the parents' income should be reported on the FAFSA. Even if the student only worked a part-time job, it's good practice to start filing taxes as a dependent and report income on the FAFSA. Unless students are making a substantial amount at a summer job, it won't affect eligibility for financial aid. If you as parents are married and live together, then you need to report both parents' incomes. If you are divorced or separated, then you report the income of the parent whom the student lives with the majority of the time. If a student splits time equally between both parents, then report the income of the parent who provides the most financial support. If a parent is remarried and is the custodial parent, then a stepparent's income will also need to be provided.

What if the parents are divorced, and the child lives with Mom but is claimed on Dad's taxes?

FAFSA only cares about the custodial parent, the parent who provides the most financial support, regardless of who claims the child on tax forms.

If a parent receives disability payments for a sibling, does that need to be reported on the FAFSA?

No, Social Security disability for a sibling is made in the name of that child and does not count as income for the parent.

What is the CSS Profile?

The CSS Profile form is a financial aid application created by the College Board that requests significantly more detail than the federal FAFSA form described earlier. It can be found on the College Board's website at student. collegeboard.org/css-financial-aid-profile.

For each college that the student sends the report to, a fee is charged, so be sure to determine if a college actually requires the form since only a small percentage of the nation's colleges and universities do. It's a bit more arduous than the FAFSA, and some schools use this information to determine how to award their own institutional need-based aid. The student still must complete the FAFSA.

What is a merit-based scholarship? Does it have to be repaid?

Merit-based awards are designed to recognize a student's talent: academic, athletic, artistic, musical, or leadership talent. In other words, the student demonstrates a quality that the college or university really values; by awarding money to the student, the college hopes to encourage enrollment. Merit-based aid is unrelated to financial need. Often the FAFSA is required before the school will post the awards to a student's financial account, but remember, these awards are not based on financial need. Be sure to check if the college has an application deadline or any other required steps in order to be considered for these awards. The best part about these scholarships is that they do not need to be repaid. But there may be renewal criteria that the student must meet in order to continue receiving the awards year after year. Read your award letters carefully.

What is a need-based award? Does it have to be repaid?

Need-based scholarships are based on either the FAFSA alone or the FAFSA and some combination of other financial aid applications such as the CSS Profile or institutional forms, the student's Estimated Family Contribution (EFC), and the cost of education at a particular school. Grants do not need to be repaid and can come from the federal government, state government, or the institutions themselves. Some need-based awards don't need to be repaid, but the student has to do something in exchange for the funding, such as the federal work-study program.

There may also be renewal criteria that the student must meet in order to continue receiving the awards year after year. Very important: read your award letters thoroughly.

What is the Net Price Calculator?

In response to a federal government mandate, the Net Price Calculator was designed several years ago to provide families with a better and truer estimate of the actual costs of a four-year education at individual institutions. It is an online tool that students and their families can use to get a rough estimate of what the true costs of four years at a given college will be. The student enters self-disclosed, unverified information (including an academic profile and financial circumstances) into the online form, and the calculator generates the estimate. Since the figures are not precise, families should not be overwhelmed by the results. Often there are additional funds available. It is important to recognize that the report does not guarantee any fixed costs since none of the information submitted by the student is verified.

I've heard that unless my family income is low, there's no point in applying for financial aid. Is that true?

Definitely not! Everyone should fill out the FAFSA form. At the very minimum, a student will learn about eligibility for federal student loans. Maybe you want to take them, maybe you don't...but there is no harm in finding out what's available to you. And in many cases, even those families who think they won't qualify for any aid are surprised at what the institutions will offer. You need to give the colleges a reason to evaluate your family for assistance, and filling out the FAFSA is the perfect way to do that.

What financial aid forms must be filled out?

At the very minimum, the FAFSA form should be completed by all students. In certain circumstances, there are additional forms that may be required, such as state applications for aid and institutional forms. Students should check with each school they are applying to in order to find out for sure.

My spouse and I are divorced. Will that impact my child getting financial aid?

When a student is considered a dependent student in the eyes of the federal government, the marital status of the student's parents does impact eligibility for financial aid. When filing the FAFSA, the student will be asked to indicate the parents' marital status. In the event that both parents are still married to each other, the income and assets for both parents are included on the FAFSA. In the event of a divorce or separation, the custodial parent must be identified. Let's say that's Mom. Mom's income and assets would appear on the form, and ex-husband Dad's income and assets would not appear anywhere on the form. The form does have a line for listing child support and household support, but the noncustodial parent's income and assets are not required on the FAFSA form. It gets a bit tricky if the custodial parent gets remarried. When the custodial parent's marital status is married, both the custodial parent and stepparent's income and assets appear on the FAFSA form. The CSS Profile form and some institutional supplemental forms will also require information about the noncustodial parent, but the FAFSA does not.

When do we find out if we're eligible for any aid?

A college or university cannot make an official offer of financial aid to a student until that student has been admitted to the institution. In some cases, you will be applying for financial aid, listing a particular college on the FAFSA form, and submitting the information before you know if your child has been accepted. The colleges cannot import the information from the FAFSA form into their systems until an acceptance has been offered. But as soon as it has been done, the college will process your financial information and prepare a financial aid award letter that details all the various types of aid that the student is eligible to receive, the cost to attend, and a list of next steps. Depending on the size of the institution, this can take anywhere from two to six weeks from the time a student has been admitted to the college and all financial aid applications have been filed.

Should I be negotiating with the colleges to try to get more aid?

Generally speaking, colleges and universities put their best foot forward right from the beginning when it comes to offering financial aid to students. It's in the school's best interest to be as affordable as possible, so they tend to offer as much as possible. That said, both people and computers make mistakes. So if you believe you have not received funding that you are entitled to, you can certainly contact the financial aid office and inquire about your eligibility. Sometimes a college may have a small number of scholarships available to assist students who are close to being able to make it work financially, so asking can't hurt; it's just not likely that big gaps will be closed through this process. Also be sure to make the college aware of any extenuating circumstances.

We can only list ten schools on the FAFSA; what if my child is applying to more schools?

If applying to more than ten schools, then list the first ten schools, and submit. Once the FAFSA has been processed, within three days, your family will receive your Student Aid Report (SAR). After receiving your SAR, you can log back into your application, erase the schools initially listed, and submit any additional schools.

What is the difference between subsidized and unsubsidized loans?

Subsidized loans are loans in which the government pays the interest on your loan while students are in school. Unsubsidized loans are loans in which interest accrues while students are still in school. Unsubsidized loans have quarterly statements, and offer the option to pay the interest at that time or capitalize the interest to the principal, meaning that the interest will be added to the total amount of the original loan.

What is work study?

Work study is a federal student aid program in which students get a job on campus and receive a paycheck for the hours worked. Work study is not guaranteed. It depends on the availability of jobs on campus. The money received from working goes directly to students and can be used for personal expenses while in school. If work study is part of a package, then your child should go to the financial aid office when first arriving on campus to secure a job placement.

What if my child receives an outside scholarship? Do we need to report it to the college?

Yes, if a student receives a scholarship outside the financial aid package from the school, then it must be reported to the school. The school can do one of three things: reduce the amount of institutional aid given, reduce the amount of loans offered, or make no changes to the financial aid package. Most of the time schools will either make no changes or reduce the amount of loans offered.

What if we don't want to take out loans or we don't want to take out the full amount?

The loan portion of a financial aid package is an offer that you have to accept, not an automatic given like grants. You don't necessarily need to accept the full amount if your family can afford not to. The majority of students do need to take out student loans to help support them through college. When evaluating your financial aid package, you need to consider your financial responsibility for the first year in addition to your financial responsibility for the full four years of attendance. Keep in mind that federal student loans have a low interest rate in addition to a variety of repayment options.

Should my child indicate on the application that we will be applying for financial aid? I heard this can be a disadvantage in admissions.

Many colleges used to be 100 percent "need blind," which means that applying for admission and being accepted had nothing to do with getting financial aid. Now a number of schools are "need aware," which means that when it's down to the wire between accepting a student who can pay the full price and one who can't, the student who does not need financial aid can be at an advantage. Always check with the financial aid office of the school if you have any questions about the aid process.

What if the financial aid package doesn't cover the full cost of attendance?

When evaluating financial aid packages, you want to look at who presents the best offer. Several factors play into the evaluation of your package. The total cost of attendance minus your Estimated Family Contribution equals your financial need. Your financial need minus your financial aid package equals your gap. Your gap is the amount of money that will have to be paid out of pocket to attend the school.

If the gap is too much, then it might make sense to reconsider options. You may be able to take out more in Parent Plus loans. Parent Plus loans are loans for parents to take out to help supplement financial aid packages.

What are extenuating circumstances and how should I let the financial aid office know about them?

If anything occurs concerning your financial situation after you submit applications (loss of job, loss of business, large medical expenses, etc.), or if there is something significant about your financial situation that cannot be reflected on forms, you need to contact the financial aid office of each school. They will usually ask you to write a letter explaining these "extenuating circumstances." Your financial aid package may be adjusted as a result.

Some Final Words of Wisdom
Must-Dos for Parents

How can I best support my child throughout the college process?

Encourage your child to be proactive and to take charge of the college process. Colleges expect it, and this will be an important factor in college admissions.

    a. Your child must complete the application, send the testing to schools, do the research, set up the college visits, ask the questions, and definitely be the one e-mailing the admissions representatives.

b. Your child must keep track of deadlines, know what materials need to be sent, and check all college accounts and e-mails from colleges. Yes, there's a great deal of work to be done after all applications/materials are submitted. Many colleges will ask students to set up accounts to check the status of their application and make sure that all materials have been received. It takes time for schools to upload transcripts and recommendations into their systems, so an account may indicate something is missing when it is there but simply not entered. It is the student's responsibility to periodically check accounts and inform the school counselor. Sometimes materials need to be resent.

c. Since Common Application essay topics are released in the spring, your child should work on the essay and résumé and have them completed and proofread before summer vacation. When the Common Application goes live on August 1 and your child registers for an account and starts to fill out the application, with the finalized essay and résumé finished, a big chunk has already been done.

You may feel overwhelmed, confused, frustrated, and wanting so much to be supportive; do not fall into the situation of doing everything for your child. Do everything you can to help your child to be proactive. You will feel better, and so will your child.

Letting Go

Why is it so difficult letting go?

In a moment filled with joy, there is still an element of sadness, when after occupying your home and your heart for eighteen years, children leave for college. But leave they must. As Dr. Jonas Salk once said, "Good parents give their children Roots and Wings. Roots to know where home is, Wings to fly away and exercise what's been taught them." Take heart in knowing that your children will take with them on their new journey everything they learned from you over the course of those eighteen years. It's okay to feel sad, but it's also okay to feel proud.

Will I only see my child during vacations?

Most parents will get to see their children during the summer months as well as during Thanksgiving,

Christmas/Hanukkah, and Easter/Passover vacations. Additionally, some colleges have fall and spring breaks, which typically give students about five days off in October and again in February or March. Students may pursue options during school breaks including internship opportunities, which may mean longer periods of not seeing one another. Remember, there are plenty of ways to visually connect with your child when college is in session, including Skype and FaceTime.

How much will leaving for college change the family dynamics?

While all families will feel the impact of a child leaving the nest, how much the dynamics will change depends on the family, including family size and closeness. The impact will typically be most keenly felt by families of only children and those who have been closely connected to their children throughout their lives. One more thought: While it is normal to want to stay in regular contact with your child during college, it is also important to give your child the opportunity to live an independent life. By letting go, you are giving your child the freedom to move forward.

My child doesn't graduate for another year (or two or three!), and yet I'm already starting to feel sad and anxious. Is this normal?

It is not only normal; it's natural. It's called anticipatory anxiety, and it refers to the impending sadness you're beginning to feel when your child leaves home. Your child will likely experience the same feelings and might begin to exhibit these feelings in unsettling and unexpected ways, including arguing with you and showing less patience. While all of this emotional upheaval is typical and even predictable, it probably won't feel at all familiar to you—at least not with the first child you send off to college.

The two lasting gifts we can give our children are roots and wings. Your child will be fine, and so will you!

NOTES

NOTES

NOTES

NOTES

NOTES

NOTES

Made in the USA
Las Vegas, NV
18 March 2022

45881070R00095